# THE
# FAREWELL
# LIGHT

ARROWSMITH
PRESS

ISBN: 979-8-9879241-6-7


Boston — New York — San Francisco — Baghdad
San Juan — Kyiv — Istanbul — Santiago, Chile
Beijing — Paris — London — Cairo — Madrid
Milan — Melbourne — Jerusalem — Darfur


11 Chestnut St.
Medford, MA 02155

arrowsmithpress@gmail.com
www.arrowsmithpress.com


The fifty-seventh Arrowsmith book
was typeset & designed by Ezra Fox
for Askold Melnyczuk & Alex Johnson
in Palatino font

Cover art by Sheila Gallagher
*The Farewell Light* © 2024, Smoke on Canvas

# THE
# FAREWELL
# LIGHT

poems by Nidia Hernández

*Translations by Rowena Hill*

*I dedicate these poems of compound times
to all the people who have been part of me.*

*I didn't mean to publish them.*

*My gratitude and love for Askold Melnyczuk, Ezra Fox,
for the Arrowsmith Press team from 2020 on.*

*To Marie Howe, Sheila Gallagher, Matthew Littell,
and to Marisela Valero.*

*To you, lovely city of Boston (I want to name you).*

*My friendship to whoever opens the pages of this book.*

# Contents

## II

## III

# IV

# INTRODUCTION

When my friend, the poet Marie Howe, wrote and asked me to meet her pal Nidia, newly arrived in Boston from Caracas via Miami, I was happy to oblige. For over three decades she hosted an award-winning radio program about the poetries of the world, *La maja desnuda*.

We met for coffee at the Fogg Museum in Cambridge. Nidia explained that the political regime in Caracas had transformed her radio station into a propaganda channel, and that for a while she'd been operating out of Spain. She also told me, in a phrase I've never forgotten, that she had devoted her life to "accumulating invisible goods." By this she meant the kind of goods that come from devoting one's self wholeheartedly to one art. If the art sometimes involves disastrous losses, it also offers immutable compensations: great poetry is language in a state of grace, inviting readers into its charmed circle. Nidia has spent a lifetime at its center, absorbing its energies.

That was three years ago. In that time, Nidia's accumulation of "invisible goods" has yielded a bimonthly series of Spanish poetry via the "Poesiaudio" feature on Arrowsmith's website, along with two books: the first English-Language edition of a selected poems by Venezuela's grandmaster, the Cervantes' Prize-winning poet, Rafael Cadenas, and an anthology, *Five Latin American Women Poets*.

It took months of prodding for Nidia to let me read some of her work. Each time I asked, she demurred. She was poetry's handmaiden, that was all. When she relented, I was thrilled and even a little astonished to discover that the invisible goods she had been incubating for decades had the heart, the depth, the wit, and the charm of the very best of this one not-so-sullen craft and art. It's a pleasure to introduce American readers to Nidia Hernández, poet, here beautifully rendered into English by the great Spanish-language translator, Rowena Hill.

*- Askold Melnyczuk*
*October 9, 2023*

# I

The Brain is just the weight of God

*Emily Dickinson*


I who love the soil
know nothing better than water

*Edith Södergran*

## Únicamente mar

Desde hace días
crece algo parecido a la nada

La blanda brújula del corazón
toma un camino de agua
luego de ir de una galaxia a otra

No puedo hacer nada
por ti o por mí
por el silencio
que el viento extiende
y lleva lejos
por la escala invertida
y perenne de los días
por el reloj que vaga
ciego
fugaz
indiferente

El radar de la memoria
rastrea
lugares
voces
bambúes
la lumbre de una casa en la montaña
un silencio que amo
y personas que te esperan

## Only sea

For days now
something like nothingness is growing

The heart's soft compass
takes a watery path
after going from one galaxy to another

I can't do anything
for you or for me
for the silence
that the wind spreads
and carries far
for the inverted and perennial
scale of the days
for the clock roaming
blind
fleeting
indifferent

The radar of memory
traces
places
voices
bamboos
the fire in a house on the mountain
a silence I love
and people waiting for you

Todo comienza a desaparecer
salvo la luz parpadeante
de las luciérnagas
y todo se vuelve posible
es posible ser una tortuguita
indefensa
frágil
sobreviviente
que vuelve al océano
sin saber nada de sus antepasados
y aún así
cumple invariable
el perímetro de sus ancestros
en el aro del mar y de la arena

Es probable
que todo sea
únicamente mar

Everything starts to vanish
except the flickering light
of the fireflies
and everything becomes possible
it's possible to be a little turtle
helpless
fragile
surviving
returning to the ocean
knowing nothing of its forebears
and even so
it invariably follows
the perimeter of its ancestors
in the circle of the sea and the sand

It's probable
that everything is
only sea

## La medida que perdimos

Deja que el viento
siga mezclando
el océano que somos

deja que construya
a su paso
la medida que perdimos

deja que hable

que dibuje los caminos
a tomar

y nos diga

qué decir

qué callar

hacia dónde ver

La amapola del silencio
hará su parte.

## The measure we lost

Let the wind
go on stirring
the ocean we are

let it form
as it passes
the measure we lost

let it speak

let it draw the roads
to be taken

and tell us

what to say

what to leave unspoken

in what direction to look

The poppy of silence
will do its part.

## Demora

Entre los árboles del bosque
cruzó un paisaje

era el tiempo
el tiempo despistado
abriéndose camino

buscando el atajo del silencio,
hablando de demoras

sintiéndose extraviado
buscando internarse en la mar

# Delay

Among the trees in a wood
a landscape passed

it was time
distracted time
opening up a way

seeking the short cut of silence
speaking of delays

feeling lost
trying to go into the sea

## Nuestra canción

El gato desmiente
el paso del tiempo

una lumbre adorna todo de rosa

yo espero silente
que el borrador de la noche
disminuya sus sombras

que todo cambie

si en el cielo
si en el espacio

un anillo de Saturno
será luna en breve

es posible que hoy
si te llamo
tu cercanía
me ponga a un paso
del delicado soplo
que reúne a las almas
y obra milagros

que llueva

que el goteo del agua
sea nuestra canción

## Our song

The cat denies
the passage of time

a glow turns everything pink

I wait in silence
for the night's eraser
to lessen its shadows

for everything to change

if in the sky
if in space

one of Saturn's rings
will soon be a moon

it's possible that today
if I call you
your nearness
will place me at one step
from the subtle breath
that unites souls
and works miracles

that it will rain

that the water dripping
will be our song

## La lluvia y el viaje

Habíamos hecho un viaje juntas
un viaje y un retorno sereno
con la amabilidad del aire
entre los árboles

Yo veía tu aura a través de la lluvia
¿o era una llovizna de luciérnagas?

Mientras conversábamos
y te miraba
entendí que ya no eras una niña

tocabas con tus dedos
el centro imaginario de las cosas
como lo hacía mi madre
cuando quería hablar de realidades

La lluvia y el viaje se fueron despidiendo
mientras tú y yo hablábamos en voz baja

poco a poco
todo se fue borrando
todo se fue borrando

# The rain and the journey

We had gone on a journey together
a journey and a serene return
with the kindness of the air
among the trees

I saw your aura through the rain
or was it a shower of fireflies?

While we conversed
and I watched you
I understood you were no longer a child

you touched with your fingers
the imaginary center of things
as my mother did
when she wanted to speak of realities

The rain and the journey were saying goodbye
while you and I spoke softly

little by little
everything was being erased
everything was being erased

## Un punto ciego

Soñaba que llovía
era de noche

Soñaba con caballos
cabalgando
que moldeaban
el sonido del viento

Todo huía

el aire soportaba
en sus hombros
el peso de una fuga

¿Qué es la eternidad
en un sueño?

¿Alguien lloraba?

¿Mi mamá
vino a visitarme
o a despedirse?

llegó de pronto
y los tiempos se trocaron

# A blind spot

I dreamed it was raining
it was night

I dreamed of horses
galloping
they were molding
the sound of the wind

Everything was fleeing

the air was bearing
on its shoulders
the weight of a flight

What is eternity
in a dream?

Was someone crying?

Had my mother
come to visit me
or to say goodbye?

she arrived suddenly
and time lost its order

me conmovió
su cara tan viejita
en sus ojos
una luz de miel
buscaba decir algo,
su pelo había desaparecido
como el horizonte
en un desierto,
sus pupilas concertaban
un punto ciego

yo sabía que ya no nos veríamos.

Me dijo
- Ay, hija-
tocó mi cara y se acostó

llevaba la ropa
de mi abuela Carmen

Me senté en el piso
como cuando era niña
y ella ordenaba
mi pelo enmarañado

Quise sonreír

pero lloré
por no tenerla
por mi silencio

her little old face
moved me,
in her eyes
a light like honey
was trying to say something,
her hair had disappeared
like the horizon
in a desert,
her pupils determined
a blind spot

I knew we wouldn't see each other again

she said
'Ah, my daughter'
she touched my face and lay down

the clothes she was wearing
belonged to my grandmother Carmen

I sat down on the floor
like when I was a child
and she was tidying
my tangled hair

I wanted to smile

but I cried
because I didn't have her
because of my silence

Lloré hasta ser agua
hasta ser mar
y comencé a nadar
hacia lo hondo
para mezclarme
con la luz de las piedras
y desaparecer

en eso
vi un mapa de tortugas
pequeñitas, azules
¿eran puntos de luz?
¿buscaban su lugar de pertenencia?
y desperté con el murmullo
de otra lluvia.

Era Neptuno
que se me aparecía
y yo le rogaba —
-quédate conmigo
tú eres el mar

I cried until I was water
until I was sea
and I began to swim
toward the depths
to blend
with the stones' light
and disappear

and then
I saw a map of turtles
tiny, blue
were they dots of light?
were they looking for the place where they belonged?
and I woke with the murmur
of another rain

It was Neptune
appearing to me
and I begged him —
'stay with me
you are the sea'

## Mi tía Roque

Entre ella y la luz
algo se demoraba

(ella es mi tía)

su visión se hacía
y deshacía en el aire

practicaba el arte y la labor
de los filamentos de la araña

entregaba cada tarde
un zurcido invisible

me llevaba consigo

por el camino
se detenía y miraba
las puntadas aéreas
de cada mariposa

iba entretejiendo
la luz mudable de la tarde
con sus hilos secretos

mi tía
con su silencio arácnido

el mismo de mi abuela Rosa

y el de todos sus hermanos

# My Aunt Roque

Between her and the light
something lingered

(she is my aunt)

a vision of her formed
and dissolved in the air

she practiced the art and labor
of spider filaments

she delivered every afternoon
an invisible darn

she took me with her

on the road
she stopped and looked
at the aerial stitches
of every butterfly

she walked interlacing
the changing light of afternoon
with her secret threads

my aunt
with her arachnid silence

the same as of my grandmother Rosa

and of all her siblings

## Refugiada

Como en el cuadro de un país lejano,
el país de una película extranjera
donde ahora vivo

estoy a solas con los árboles
refugiada
entre sus copas

Toco la lluvia que cae sobre ellos
humedeciendo su corteza
dibujando planetas
continentes
sobre sus troncos
en la madera de un idioma
donde todo nace
y vuelve a renacer
donde la condición foránea
es un arbusto
que con su movimiento
dice -Ven.

# A refugee

Like in a painting of a distant country
the country in a foreign film
where I live now

I'm alone with the trees
a refugee
among their crowns

I touch the rain that falls on them
moistening their bark
drawing planets
continents
on their trunks
on the wood of a language
where everything is born
and reborn again
where the foreign condition
is a bush
that with its movement
says 'come'.

# Río Turbio

Mientras miraba
un río en una película
pensaba en todo
lo que se ha ido
como el agua

todo huía con el río

El mundo era
una flor pasajera
una flecha
que borraba
la calidez del instante
en que un gato aparece

Busqué en la memoria
un río de mi infancia
el río de mi mamá
"El río turbio"
de su pueblo
en Venezuela.

Me detuve ante
el silencio de tanta lejanía
de mi país borrándose
y de ese río turbio de mis tías
turbio como mis ojos
en estos días
sin lentes
y sin optometrista

# Río Turbio

While I watched
a river in a film
I thought about everything
that has gone
like the water

everything was fleeing with the river

The world was
an ephemeral flower
an arrow
that erased
the warmth of the moment
when a cat appears

I searched in memory
for a river from my childhood
my mother's river
'the muddy river'
in her village
in Venezuela.

I stopped in front of
the silence of all that distance
of my country being erased
and of my aunts' muddy river
muddy like my eyes
these days
without glasses
and without an optometrist

# El amor familiar

Mi abuela Rosa
la invisible
la lejana
de cálida mirada
circunspecta
enseñándonos
que la distancia
era el amor familiar

no fue largo su viaje
pero anduvo y anduvo
y conformó desde niña
el vecindario nómada mundial

Mi abuela Carmen
nos amó en silencio
siempre asertiva
dibujó para todos
una cruz en el aire
mientras bendecía a su hijo
que murió antes que ella
"no me abracen"
nos dijo a todos

A mis abuelos
nunca los conocí

## Family love

My grandmother Rosa
invisible
remote
with her warm gaze
discreet
teaching us
how distance
was family love

her journey wasn't long
but she went and she went
and belonged from her childhood
to the world nomad neighborhood

My grandmother Carmen
loved us in silence
always assertive
she drew for all of us
a cross in the air
while she blessed her son
who died before her
'Don't hug me'
she told all of us

My grandfathers
I never knew

Los deletreo
en las canciones antiguas
en los ojos de los extranjeros

a veces entro en sus miradas
algo suspendido gira
y dibuja la luz del polvo
que vemos en los árboles

a veces siento
que si hablo con ellos
soy un prado.

I spell them
in the old songs
in the eyes of foreigners

sometimes I enter their gaze
something suspended spins
and sketches the light in the dust

that we see in the trees
sometimes I feel
that if I speak with them
I'm a meadow.

## Loba, mi perra

Estaba regando los cambures
era muy tarde
y casi no veía

Sujetaba la manguera
de pronto
la fuerza del agua
me suspendió en el aire
en forma circular
comencé a dar vueltas

Recuerdo que intentaba orientarme
por los sonidos del agua
en los árboles

Loba, mi pastor
me acompañaba
hacía lo mismo a mi lado
éramos satélites la una de la otra

Loba
que fue mi guía
volvió para decirme
que aún tenemos nuestro reino

Al día siguiente
el jardín
tenía la mirada
de un bosque
cuando llueve

## Loba, my dog

I was watering the banana plants
it was very late
and I could hardly see

I was holding the hose
suddenly
the water's force
suspended me in the air
in a circle
I started to go round

I remember I tried to orient myself
by the sound of the water
in the trees

Loba my shepherd
was with me
doing the same beside me
we were satellites of each other

Loba
who was my guide
came back to tell me
we still have our kingdom

The next day
the garden
had the gaze
of a wood
when it rains

## María Fernanda

Evitando reunir tus fotos
cierro una puerta
la nieve comienza a caer

Es enero
y los recuerdos
descienden
aleatorios
blandos
como copos

desde un punto curvo
el viento los dispersa

No puedo ir hasta ti
no son las fotografías
que baraja el *inconsciente*
(palabra que amabas,
junto a dramaturgia,
Shakespeare)

No pude atravesar
la telaraña de piedra
que fuiste tejiendo

Me fui por mucho tiempo
oh corazón
oh alma
oh desconsuelo...

## María Fernanda

Avoiding gathering up your photos
I close a door
the snow starts to fall

It's January
and memories
descend
at random
soft
as snowflakes

from a curved spot
the wind disperses them

I can't go to you
it's not the photos
that the *unconscious* shuffles
(a word you loved
together with dramaturgy
Shakespeare)

I couldn't cross
the stone spider's web
that you were weaving

I went away for a long time
oh heart
oh soul
oh desolation...

## Hogar

Un reloj apuntaba
hacia el lugar
donde un aro incandescente
tocaba las sombras

era mi cuarto
que flotaba en la noche

mi cuarto
defendiéndome de mí misma

mi cuarto oscuro
donde escondo
las pirámides que sueño

era mi cuarto de segundo
para estar en todas partes

para llegar a ti

para tocarte

para oír tu voz

era la irrealidad
mi verdadero cuarto

la inmensa irrealidad

mi único hogar

# Home

A clock pointed
toward the place
where an incandescent ring
touched the shadows

it was my room
floating in the night

my room
defending me from myself

my dark room
where I hide
the pyramids I dream

it was the space of a second
to be everywhere

to reach you

to touch you

to hear your voice

it was unreality
my true room

immense unreality

my only home

## Algo que saber

La serenidad cambia de turno

quiero ir con ella

con su tiempo despistado
con su oscilante andar
con su cara de niña

hoy supe que ibas a morir

¿hay algo que saber?
acerca del miedo
el pensamiento de la lluvia
la tristeza?

la serenidad
habla con la distancia

caminan juntas

se esfuman

## Something to know

Serenity changes shifts

I want to go with it

with its distracted rhythm
with its swaying walk
with its little girl's face

today I found out you were going to die

is there something to know?
about the fear
the thoughts of the rain
sadness?

serenity
talks with the distance

they walk together

they vanish

## El incendio en la montaña

Comencé a oír el fuego
y cómo su cabellera de oro
se iba expandiendo

Había una gran sequía

El fuego en los árboles
en los bambúes

¿dónde están los perros?

¿dónde el señor Mario?

Salí con una olla llena de agua
la más grande que podía cargar

el fuego abría enorme sus brazos
desplegaba sus picos impacientes
silbaba un remolino en el viento

sus llamas se elevaban infinitas
tenían el color de las estrellas

vi el fuego por dentro
no podía creer lo que miraba

lo vi a los ojos

# The fire on the mountain

I began to hear the fire
and how its golden mane
was spreading

There was a great drought

The fire in the trees
in the bamboos

where are the dogs?

where is señor Mario?

I went out with a pot full of water
the biggest I could carry

the fire was spreading its huge arms wide
unfurling its impatient peaks
a vortex was whistling in the wind

its flames rose to infinity
they were the color of the stars

I saw the fire inside
I couldn't believe what I was seeing

I looked into its eyes

por un instante se detuvo

él también me vio

desde mi pequeñez le dije
-eres hermoso

ya no importaba
si se quemaba todo
o si tenía algo
que aprender de las cenizas

-eres un Rey
haz lo que quieras

Recogió el vacío con sus cuarzos
giró sobre sí mismo
y se alejó como un relámpago

sus llamas
su corona
tal vez se condolieron
de mi agua y de mi olla

for an instant it stopped

it saw me too

out of my smallness I said
'you are beautiful'

it no longer mattered
if everything burned
or if I had something
to learn from the ashes

'you are a king
do as you like'

It picked up the void with its quartzes
turned on itself
and fled away like lightning

its flames
its corona
maybe felt sorry
for my water and my pot

## Chrysanthemums, 17 de Diciembre

Hay una reverencia
del ave hacia los árboles

en el lago
el agua palpita bajo el hielo
el firmamento, las nubes
y una flor de invierno, se asoman a su puerto

un pájaro azul
le habla a otro con su canto

¿cantará para ti?

las orugas esperan

Nada ha cambiado
todo ha cambiado

Un mirlo dibuja brújulas
que soplan primaveras
a quien llora en invierno

Hoy es tu cumpleaños
no podré abrazarte

pero Camelias, Crisantemos, Amarilis,
Ciclamen, Prímulas, Narcisos
Flor de cerezo

Y Pensamientos para ti

# Chrysanthemums, 17th December

There's a reverence
of the bird toward the trees

in the lake
the water throbs under the ice
the sky the clouds
and a winter flower glimpse their port

a blue bird
speaks to another with its song

will it sing for you?

caterpillars wait

Nothing has changed
everything has changed

A blackbird sketches compasses
they breathe springtime
to someone weeping in winter

Today is your birthday
I won't be able to hug you

but Camelias, Chrysanthemums,
Primulas, Daffodils,
Cherry Blossoms and

Pansies for you

## Hermanas

Las ondas de la lluvia
hilan memorias

miro el cielo
sus gotas me acercan
un recuerdo infantil

una niña que mira
a su hermana mayor
una niña que mira a otra niña

no sabe aún que el tiempo
transportará partidas
distancias
desencuentros

Solo es una niña
con su hermana
cantando una canción

## Sisters

The waves of rain
spin memories

I look at the sky
its drops bring me
a memory of childhood

a little girl looking
at her older sister
a little girl looking at another little girl

she doesn't know yet that time
will bring departures
distances
failed meetings

She is just a little girl
with her sister
singing a song

## Todo se escapa

Solo por ver sus ojos
correría millones de kilómetros,
solo por ver sus ojos

Trasladarme de un reino a otro
no bastará para alcanzarla

Todo se escapa,
el diámetro del aire
duplica el zurcido
cada vez menos invisible
de la soledad.

Por el viento
viajan sus señales

-No la veré más-
 no hay reproches

# Everything escapes

Just to see her eyes
I would run millions of kilometers
just to see her eyes

Moving from one realm to another
won't suffice to reach her

Everything escapes
the diameter of the air
doubles the less and less invisible
stitching of loneliness.

On the wind
her signals travel

-I won't see her again-
there's no reproach

# Nanda

Vestía de blanco
venía de la muerte

lucía más joven
que la última vez que la vi

Le pregunté
-¿de dónde vienes?
contestó
-no va a estar bien,
la vi muy mal,
me dio esto

sacó de su bolso un ovillo
y pedazos de un rompecabezas

no quería seguir buscando
todo la maltrataba

se sentó con su pelo rapado bajo un árbol

la incertidumbre no mentía
la realidad desde siempre
se devora a sí misma

# Nanda

She was dressed in white
she came from death

she looked younger
than the last time I saw her

I asked her
'where are you coming from?'
she answered
'it's not going to be all right,'
she looked very bad,
she gave me this

she took out of her bag a ball of wool
and pieces of a jigsaw puzzle

she didn't want to go on seeking
everything hurt her

she sat down with her shaven head under a tree

uncertainty doesn't lie
reality has always
devoured itself

Una tarde de abril nos despedimos
sin decir adiós
El silencio era un país lejano
que habíamos elegido

Ella bajaba escaleras
el abismo las subía

yo miraba y miraba
la cuerda floja del tiempo

Vestía de blanco
venía de la muerte.

One April afternoon we saw each other off
without saying goodbye
Silence was a distant country
that we'd chosen

She was going down steps
the abyss was moving up

I looked and looked
at the tightrope of time

She was wearing white
she came from death.

# II

All I have is the feeling suspended from everything
With eternity floating over the mountains

*Sophia de Mello Breyner*

-children, the ocean, wildlife, Bach
—man is a strange animal

*Blanca Varela*

## Helada

Ven conmigo
la nieve es un sueño

una percepción

una caída

la memoria
de una bandada de gardenias
que van rotándose
a sí mismas
en el aire.

dame la mano

una helada cae sobre el mundo

su luz
es el acoplamiento
de lo impermanente
con el agua del cielo

Háblame,
dime algo
caminemos

entendamos
que la introspección
es la más suave
y dulce compañía.

## Freeze

Come with me
the snow is a dream

a perception

a fall

the memory
of a flock of gardenias
rotating
on themselves
in the air.

give me your hand

a freeze is falling over the world

its light
is the coupling
of impermanence
with the water in the sky

Speak to me,
tell me something
let's walk

let's understand
that introspection
is the gentlest
and sweetest company.

# El silencio persiste

El silencio persiste
cabalga sus aguas
mientras la luna
mueve sus picos
y el sol
escanea el cielo
con un ramo de luces
que reúnen
lugares olvidados

Pero algo se escapa
y lentamente
quien observa
es besado por la luna
y el que calla
es llevado por la noche
a sus montañas

## Silence persists

Silence persists
rides its waters
while the moon
moves its peaks
the sun
scans the sky
with a branch of lights
that bring together
forgotten places

But something escapes
and slowly
the one who observes
is kissed by the moon
and the one who remains silent
is carried by the night
to its mountains

## Secreto

¿Quién puede mirar
fijamente una estrella
desde el anochecer
hasta el amanecer
sin mirar a los lados
para no ver
todo lo que se fue?

Una ardilla en el árbol
extrae diligente un fruto

un búho inmóvil
planea lo que pasó hace siglos

la luna cuelga del cielo
su reflejo

¿quién puede con sólo desearlo
morar en esa cámara secreta?

La luna sumergida en el lago
titila esa ecuación

## Secret

Who can stare
at a star
from nightfall
until dawn
without glancing aside
so as not to see
all that's gone?

A squirrel in the tree
diligently extracts a fruit

a motionless owl
plans what happened centuries ago

the moon hangs her reflection
from the sky

Who can by just wishing
dwell in this secret chamber?

The moon sunk in the lake
flickers that equation

# Desde la luna

Recordar desde la luna

cómo la lentitud
cruza la tarde
en forma de gaviota

cómo va frisando
la silueta de estos días
en los que nunca estás

premeditar
una manera de rondarte

besar
el polen del silencio

acariciar
cada fase
de la luna azul

# From the moon

Remembering from the moon

how slowness
crosses the evening
in the shape of a seagull

how it coats
the contour of these days
when you are never there

premeditating
a way of encircling you

kissing
the pollen of silence

caressing
each phase
of the blue moon

## El mar y la nada

Lo que creí perdido
está en la luz de este amanecer

No estoy sola
la nada es solo la nada

el mar me habla
lo escucho y asiento

Toco la distancia
el horizonte disuelto en el océano
moja mis dedos

Digo tu nombre
hay un viaje por hacer
astros que contemplar

entro al mar
en cámara lenta

## The sea and emptiness

What I thought lost
is in the light of this dawn

I'm not alone
emptiness is only emptiness

the sea speaks to me
I listen and assent

I touch distance
the horizon dissolved in the ocean
wets my fingers

I say your name
there's a journey to be taken
stars to contemplate

I walk into the sea
in slow motion

## Llovizna

Con entrar en la noche
lo hubiéramos sabido

guiadas por la orientación
de una nebulosa

se está en la certidumbre
cuando vemos desde el cielo

todo se va
el relámpago,
sus llamaradas

nos queda
entregarse a la lluvia
pasar en forma de arena
a cuenta gota

estar serena

llorar a veces

ser llovizna

oír una canción

## Drizzle

Entering the night
we would have known it

guided by the orientation
of a nebula

we inhabit certainty
when we see from the sky

everything goes away
the lightning
its flashes

what's left to us
yielding to the rain
passing as sand
from a dropper

being serene

weeping sometimes

being drizzle

hearing a song

## Acero y gravedad

Te esfumaste
no existes

Anunciaste en tus ojos
paraísos ingrávidos

Ahora
mi corazón
arrastra ese peso
de acero

## Steel and gravity

You vanished
you don't exist

You announced in your eyes
weightless paradises

Now
my heart
is dragging that weight
of steel

# El manuscrito de la lluvia

Eres irreal
–me dices

te pregunto
-¿escribir en el agua es ilusorio?
(tú sonríes)

Te entrego
el manuscrito de la lluvia

lo  extraviarás
el próximo cuarto de segundo.

# The manuscript of the rain

'You are unreal'
you tell me

I ask you
'is writing on water illusory?'
(you smile)

I hand over to you
the manuscript of the rain

you will lose it
in the next quarter second.

## El paisaje del tiempo

No era la elíptica de tu mirada
que describía
el paisaje del tiempo

no eran dos chicas perfumadas
tomadas de la mano

no era el anochecer
ni tu ausencia
ni la horizontalidad
que se asomaba

Una plegaria
tocaba la puerta
y nadie quería abrir

afuera todo decía adiós
salvo el sol que prometía
volver todos los días

afuera
todo decía adiós

# Time's landscape

It was not the ellipse of your gaze
that described
time's landscape

it was not two scented girls
holding hands

it was not nightfall
nor your absence
nor horizontality
breaking out

A prayer
knocked on the door
and no one wanted to open it

outside everything was saying goodbye
except the sun that promised
to come back every day

outside
everything was saying goodbye

## El Cielo Subsiguiente

Las horas pasan lentamente

todo cambia de lugar

un secreto rueda sobre sí

la verdadera soledad

el cielo subsiguiente

ya nada es lo mismo

lo bello toca fondo

qué nostalgia

lo triste es un barco

las mariposas
también cambian de lugar

la velocidad de las estrellas

el encuentro de dos mundos

mi dispersión escondiéndome

nadie se ha ido

el horizonte dobla el atardecer
es mi espejo

# The following sky

The hours pass slowly

everything changes place

a secret rolls over

the true solitude

the following sky

already nothing is the same

beauty touches rock bottom

what nostalgia

sadness is a boat

butterflies
change place too

the speed of the stars

the meeting of two worlds

my dispersal hiding me

no one has left

the horizon doubles the sunset
it's my mirror

## Mare Imbrium

Luna
¿qué me dices esta noche
de cuarto creciente?

¿qué me dices
en un cuarto de segundo?

cuando soñamos
nos mezclamos con tu sombra

menguante y extranjera

con el agua velada
de tu manto lunar

cuando soñamos

giramos contigo
buscando descansar
en tu almohada de espuma
donde somos ecuaciones
donde somos
aros del espacio

## Mare Imbrium

Moon
what are you telling me on
your crescent
quarter night?

what are you telling me
in a quarter of a second?

when we dream
we merge with your shadow

waning and foreign

with the veiled water
of your lunar mantle

when we dream

we spin with you
trying to rest
on your foam pillow
where we are equations
where we are
rings in space

## La nada

La nada me dio su mano
la toqué

La nada es un atardecer
que quiere huir
y se evapora
levemente en rosa

# Nothingness

Nothingness gave me its hand
I touched it

Nothing is a twilight
that wants to flee
and evaporates
lightly in pink

## Un caballo

En agosto de 2022
va un hombre a caballo
por un parque de Boston

los ojos del animal
son un lago intranquilo
que cabalga
dentro de una canción

Algo tiene que ser verdad

pero contigo
no lo sé

no es posible saber
si alguna vez solo hubo azar

si alguien sostenía
la luz del mundo,
o era el sol dibujando
una columna en el agua
que todos podíamos tocar

Yo solo sé
que en tus ojos
vi un caballo
que quería jugar.

# A horse

In August 2022
a man on a horse is going
through a park in Boston

the animal's eyes
are a restless lake
riding
inside a song

Something has to be true

but with you
I don't know

it's not possible to know
if at any time there was only chance

if someone sustained
light in the world
or it was the sun drawing
a column in the water
that all of us could touch

I only know
that in your eyes
I saw a horse
that wanted to play.

# III

the nights exist, the nightshade exists
the night side, the cloak of namelessness exists

*Inger Christensen*

# I love confusion

*Para Sheila Gallagher*

*¿After?*
*¿Before?*

Es *before*
no, *es after*

-¿por qué te confundes?

-Deja que me confunda,
I love confusion

Sheila se ríe
mientras sigue mirando
un búho entre los árboles

hipnotizados
Sheila y el búho
se intercambian
pareceres celestes
en una misma lengua

el humo de su té
se une a la neblina
y ambos se entienden

La confusión
me mira amable
sabe que todos la evitan

Yo no lo hago.

# I love confusion

*For Sheila Gallagher*

*After?*
*Before?*

It's *before*
no, *it's after*

why do you get confused?

'Let me get confused,
I love confusion'

Sheila laughs
while she goes on looking
at an owl among the trees

hypnotized
Sheila and the owl
exchange
celestial opinions
in the same language

The smoke from their tea
blends with the mist
and they understand each other

Confusion
looks at me kindly
it knows that everyone avoids it

I don't.

## La cueva de una misma lengua

Cuando me encierro
y mi corazón comienza a modularse

cuando la oscuridad lo abraza todo
y puedo dormir sin sobresalto
en la cueva de una misma lengua

cuando lo que transcurre incontenible:

el flujo del mar

las arenas del desierto de Sahara
nutriendo cada año
a los Bosques Amazónicos

el halo postergado del ayer
titilando en la inconsciencia

cuando todo se esfuma
los países se confunden
el mar vuelve a ser nuestro reloj

entonces podemos
voltearnos como olas.

# The cave of one same tongue

When I shut myself in
and my heart begins to modulate

when darkness embraces all
and I can sleep without startling
in the cave of one same tongue

when what goes on unstoppably:

the sea's flow

the sands of the Sahara desert
nourishing every year
the Amazon forests

yesterday's postponed aura
glimmering in the unconscious

when everything blurs
countries are confused
the sea becomes our clock again

then we can
turn over like waves.

## Traducción

Ahora que hablo con Neptuno
y transo líneas con él,
ahora que apago la luz
para ver lo que queda
en el lado oscuro de la luna

ahora que la memoria
no busca algo a punto de perderse
ahora que doy traspiés en otro idioma
contando y descontando palabras

ahora y en la hora del alma
que todo lo adivina
no hay duda
de que todo volverá

Eso dice
mi traducción imaginaria
de una canción que estoy oyendo

# Translation

Now that I'm speaking with Neptune
and discussing lines with him
now that I'm turning out the light
to see what's left
on the dark side of the moon

now that memory
isn't looking for something about to be lost
now that I'm stumbling in a different language
counting and discounting words

now and in the hour of the soul
that divines everything
there is no doubt
everything will return

That's what it says
my imaginary translation
of a song I'm listening to

## El mismo idioma

Aunque soy una foránea
en un país ajeno
el relato de mi alma
puede convivir
con todos los idiomas

esto confirma
que alguien
puede traducir
la oscuridad
el abismo
la orfandad
y la luz que se posa en el agua
aún si estás
desorientada en otra lengua

no entenderse
no hablar el mismo idioma
es la constante

en nuestras bocas
tu lengua
se acomoda entre tus dientes
para decir *thank you*
y la mía toca su cielo
con la palabra *oral*

## The same language

Although I'm a foreigner
in an alien country
my soul's story
can cohabit
with all languages

this confirms
that someone
can translate
darkness
the abyss
orphanhood
and the light that settles on the water
even if they are
disoriented in a different tongue

not understanding each other
not speaking the same language
is the constant

in our mouths
your tongue
fits between your teeth
to say *thank you*
and mine touches its roof
with the word *oral*

## Una rosa azul

Caminaba por un mundo foráneo
cuyo eco se redoblaba
en una lengua
que quería abrazar
pero que estaba afuera,
y no había manera de alcanzarla

Cada palabra duplicaba su abismo
hasta que uno de sus hilos
se fue soltando
y escaló la luna

Vi cómo subía
mientras yo ascendía
hacia una traducción incomprensible

Era el lenguaje que cedía
su horizonte
su música

Su gramática:
una rosa azul

## Blue rose

I was walking through a foreign world
whose echo doubled
in a language
that I wanted to embrace
but it was outside
and there was no way to reach it

Each word duplicated its abyss
until one of its threads
came loose
and climbed the moon

I saw how it went up
while I ascended
toward an incomprehensible translation

It was language that was yielding
its horizon
its music

Its grammar:
a blue rose

## La pregunta en otro idioma

Mientras arrastro
la maleta sin ruedas
de estos tiempos
y cambio la velocidad
de mi canción
para asimilar mi viaje
y poner los pies
bien puestos
tanto en la tierra
como en el cielo,
se me acerca una señora
y me pregunta
por un cruce de caminos

Con su dedo
señala la distancia
entre nosotras y el lago

El lago que vemos detenido
no deja de titilar

Nunca entendí
la pregunta en otro idioma

# The question in a different language

While I drag
the wheelless suitcase
of these times
and change gears
in my song
to assimilate my journey
and place my feet
firmly
both on earth
and in the sky
a lady approaches me
and asks me
about a crossroads

With her finger
she points to the distance
between us and the lake

The lake we see paused
doesn't stop shimmering

I never understood
the question in a different language

## Walt Whitman

El cielo doblemente imaginario
deja ver la erosión
detrás del claro de la tarde

Si es que algo estuviera perdido
busco al poeta
unitario
ocioso
vagabundo

La humedad de sus hojas
abren la cadencia
del secreto del mundo

¿Será que había algo
que él no prefigurara?

Los pistilos pensativos de la noche
el sol ambiguo y profundo
la hierba
la gracia

Al borde del agujero negro
pero ante un mar de lilas
sentada sobre la hierba
en el *arboretum*
toco su barba
su barba venerable
la acaricio y me enmiendo
la barba de Walt Whitman
con más tiempo
que todas las estrellas.

## Walt Whitman

The doubly imaginary sky
reveals the erosion
behind the clarity of afternoon

If something should happen to be lost
I seek the one
idle
vagrant
poet

The moisture of his leaves
opens the cadence
of the world's secrets

Could it be there's something
he didn't anticipate?

The thoughtful pistils of the night
the ambiguous deep sun
grass
grace

At the edge of the black hole
but in front of a sea of lilacs
sitting on the grass
in the arboretum
I touch his beard
his venerable beard
I stroke it and I amend myself
Walt Whitman's beard
longer lasting
than all the stars.

## Edith Sitwell

La noche titila su luz
sobre un poema de Edith Sitwell
en el que habla de una iglesia
destruida por la guerra

todo es lluvia
el fuego que cae del cielo
la campana
la iglesia y la sangre
el salmo susurrado al pie del crucifijo
el polvo que detalla el fin del mundo

vuelvo a mis cosas
afuera también llueve
busco de nuevo el poema
y a la poeta
para que juntas
miremos el cielo

le pregunto
por su ropa isabelina

ella me mira
quiere decirme algo
con las gotas de la lluvia

la sigo del lado de los truenos
y alzo su libro

nos mojamos

quiero acompañar a la poeta

## Edith Sitwell

The night shimmers its light
over a poem by Edith Sitwell
in which she speaks of a church
destroyed by the war

all is rain
the fire that falls from the sky
the bell
the church and the blood
the psalm whispered at the foot of the cross
the dust detailing the end of the world

I go back to my affairs
outside it's raining too
I look up the poem again
and the poet
so that together
we can gaze at the sky

I ask her
about her Elizabethan clothes

she looks at me
wants to say something
in the drops of rain

I follow her on the thunder's side
and lift her book

we get wet

I want to keep the poet company

## Jorge Eielson

¿Eres consciente
de que en tus sueños
la noción del tiempo
las vueltas del espacio
el mar y el cielo
se encuentran
en un mismo talismán?

Hoy al despertar
me traje de la noche
la sonrisa de un poeta
*La sonrisa de Leonardo*
*Es una rosa cansada*
Diría, Eielson

Soñé con Jorge Eielson
lo conocí en Caracas en el 85

Nos saludábamos

Éramos muy amigos
yo estaba alegre de verlo
nos unían mil hilos
me veía atento
yo también lo escrutaba

# Jorge Eielson

Are you aware
that in your dreams
the notion of time
the loops of space
the sea and the sky
are to be found
in the same talisman?

Today on waking
I brought with me from the night
the smile of a poet
*Leonardo's smile*
*is a tired rose*
Eielson would say

I dreamt of Jorge Eielson
I met him in Caracas in '85

We greeted each other

We were great friends
I was happy to see him
a thousand threads joined us
he looked at me carefully
I studied him too

su mirada peruana
se abría sobre mí
como el sol en los bosques
al anochecer

Al despertar
seguía conmigo
a través de una metáfora

una luz azul
que trasladaba
los cielos a la tierra
en un talismán

me reuní con el poeta
en la vida y en los sueños

luego busqué sus libros
sus cartas
sus poemas

y lloré por sus versos:

"Los verdaderos poetas aparecen
sin que nadie se dé cuenta"

his Peruvian gaze
opened on to me
like the sun in woods
at nightfall

When I woke
he was still with me
through a metaphor

a blue light
that transferred
the heavens to earth
in a talisman

I met the poet
in life and in dreams

later I found his books
his letters
his poems

and I cried over his lines:

"True poets appear
without anyone noticing"

# IV

Walk the road backward,
Thick with trees, out through to pasture
Where the bucket hangs ready to fill

*Sophie Cabot Black*

## Venus, Júpiter & la Luna, Febrero, 2023

Cerca de la luna
Venus y Júpiter
titilan enlazados
por un aro visible

creando el temblor
de los presagios

la luna
ensaya nuevas faces
mientras mueve las arenas
de su cráter rosado

desde la distancia vemos
los dones del cielo en la tierra

algo viaja
eternamente
hacia el vacío

esa escala
que llamamos sombra

# Venus, Jupiter & the moon, February, 2023

Near the moon
Venus and Jupiter
twinkle bound together
by a visible ring

creating a tremor
of omens

the moon
tries out new phases
while she shifts the sands
of her rosy crater

from the distance we see
the gifts of sky on earth

something is traveling
eternally
toward the void

that gradation
that we call shadow

# Aprendizaje

Oye cómo va bajando
lentamente la nieve
cómo va goteando
su canción

oye cómo se desplaza
ondulándose
con su capa blanca
indiferente al mundo

no quiere llegar
se demora
sobre sí misma

ahora la toco
se desvanece

pero antes
rueda en un espejo

me gusta oírla
paciente
leal
la nieve
te enseña a esperar

## Learning

Listen how the snow
is descending slowly
how it's dripping
its song

listen how it moves
rippling
in its white cape
indifferent to the world

it doesn't want to arrive
it lingers
over itself

now I touch it
it vanishes

but before
it swirls in a mirror

I like to hear it
patient
loyal
the snow
teaches you to wait

## La Luna Paleolítica

Es temprano
en la calle llena de gente
no hay señal de sosiego

Todos somos extranjeros
por la forma en que nos movemos
tratando de igualar el eje
de rotación de este lugar

Un señor se asoma a los locales
y termina con cara de extraviado

El agujero de la equivocación lo acompaña
él trata de burlarlo
pero a lo mejor es el agujero negro

Yo busco el numero 1718 con el tiempo contado
en esta hermosa ciudad cuyas casas
son las de una película

La prisa aquí tiene el sentido
de un barco postergado
con pasajeros que no quieren llegar
porque ya no tienen casa

Si fuera de noche
las mensurables fases
de la luna
y la luna más larga
la luna Paleolítica
serían nuestro hogar

## The Paleolithic Moon

It's early
in the street crowded with people
there's no sign of calm

We're all foreigners
from the way we move
trying to match the rotational
axis of this place

A man looks into the shops
and ends up with a lost expression

The hole of being in error goes with him
he tries to outwit it
but maybe it's the black hole

I look for the number 1718 running out of time
in this beautiful city where the houses
are from a film

Haste here has the meaning
of a delayed ship
with passengers that don't want to arrive
because they no longer have homes

If it was night
the measurable phases
of the moon
and the longest moon
the Paleolithic moon
would be our home

# Miopía

Pensé que caminaba
lentamente
en realidad flotaba

quería posarme
pero no podía

estaba en el fondo del mar
su corriente
me llevaba a sus cuevas

en la curva del agua
veía el tiempo
lo tocaba

nadé una milla de agua
con la flotabilidad
de las tortugas
y la imantación
que ellas usan
para volver a sus lugares

Me valí de la miopía

me concentré
en las esponjas,
en las algas,

# Myopia

I thought I was walking
slowly
in reality I was floating

I wanted to settle
but I couldn't

I was on the sea bottom
the current
was carrying me to its caves

in the curve of the water
I was looking at time
I was touching it

I swam a mile of water
as buoyant
as turtles
and magnetized
like they are
to return to their places

I put to use my myopia

I concentrated
on the sponges,
on the algae,

en mi medusa interna
y pude unirme
a mi propio extravío

Ahora
sé maniobrar
la luz que se fuga
del sol más denso

on my inner jellyfish
and I was able to join with
my own lostness

Now
I know how to handle
the light that escapes
the densest sun

## El Gato Argon

Alguien acaricia un gato
y la lana de Argon se distiende
donde sea que esté

Recuerdo cómo entornaba
su atigrado mirar
y cómo saltaba
apareciendo
el balance en el mundo

Algo se despide
por eso pienso en Argon
que partió lentamente
transportando en su lomo
la luz del adiós

Un secreto leopardo
se llevó consigo

El centro de sus ojos
sigue siendo mi casa
donde puedo
premeditar horizontes
una piedra angular
y voltear los espejos del sol
hacia la luna

Extraño su malicia
y su peso del aire

Aún lo espero
para dormir con él

## Argon the cat

Someone is stroking a cat
and Argon's fur fluffs up
wherever he is

I remember how he half closed
his tiger's eyes
how he jumped
revealing
the balance in the world

Something takes leave
so I think of Argon
who left slowly
carrying on his back
the farewell light

A secret leopard
he took with him

The center of his eyes
is still my home
where I can
premeditate horizons
a corner stone
and turn the sun's mirrors
toward the moon

I miss his mischief
and his weight of air

I still wait for him
to sleep with him

## Árbol

El músico cuando era niño
enterró su corazón
dentro de un árbol

Su abuela le decía
que su madre no estaba
porque vivía en una selva

Hoy va con su trompeta
traduciendo algo parecido
al latido del bosque

lento
como la lluvia
en un sueño

solfeando
el swing
de la inconsciencia

## Tree

The musician when he was a boy
buried his heart
inside a tree

His grandmother told him
his mother was not there
because she lived in a forest

Today he goes translating
with his trumpet something akin
to the heartbeat of a wood

slow
like the rain
in a dream

playing scales
on the swing
of unawareness

## Miami Book Fair 2016

Era un muchacho
de mirada perdida

llegó tarde
despistado

Le dije a mis amigas
-Él es un poeta
(no todos lo eran)

un poeta y un árbol
siempre son intercambiables

su mirada viajaba
como un tren sin destino

un chico de ojos grises
parpadeando abismos

¿lo encapsulaba
el anillo de Saturno?

Yo lo quería abrazar
por su silencio
que traspasaba piedras

¿conoció a su madre?
¿tenía una hermana perdida?

# Miami Book Fair, 2016

He was a boy
with a blank stare

he arrived late
disoriented

I told my girlfriends
'He's a poet'
(not all of them were)

a poet and a tree
are always interchangeable

his gaze traveled
like a train with no destination

a boy with grey eyes
blinking abysses

was he encapsulated
in a ring of Saturn?

I wanted to hug him
for his silence
that pierced stones

did he know his mother?
did he have a lost sister?

¿cuál era su tristeza
que atravesaba océanos
y llegaba intacta
a aparearse con un lobo
que aullaba
y aullaba?

¿llevaba en sus hombros
un gorrión que lloraba?

what was his sadness
that crossed oceans
and arrived intact
to couple with a wolf
that howled
and howled?

was he carrying on his shoulder
a weeping sparrow?

## Jamaica Pond

La carrera del mundo
es una mujer trotando
con un dolor en el pie derecho
que repentinamente
aparece del otro lado del mundo

su gran entrenamiento
es la brisa viajando
a gran velocidad
entre los árboles
y el mensaje de los arándanos
dibujándose en el lago

hablo de un oasis
un gran bosque
donde corremos
con las flores y las aves

el viento va soltando sus secretos
que se amalgaman con los nuestros

dos cisnes se acomodan
en la almohada del agua

el paisaje hace parodias
en sentido contrario
para los fotógrafos

## Jamaica Pond

The world race
is a woman jogging
with a pain in her right foot
who suddenly
appears on the other side of the world

her great training
is the breeze traveling
at high speed
through the trees
and the message of the bilberries
being drawn on the lake

I'm speaking of an oasis
a big wood
where we run
with the flowers and the birds

the wind gradually gives up its secrets
which blend with ours

two swans settle
on the pillow of the water

the landscape makes parodies
in the opposite direction
for photographers

la luna a veces se queda
la vemos distante,
ajena a la globalización
de su cráter rosado

De pronto
todos nos detenemos por un estruendo,
una revuelta de aves contra un halcón
clavado inamovible en un árbol
que se jacta del acero de sus ojos

los pajaritos angustiados
se tiran sobre él

"Estás asustando a mi bebé"
parecen decirle
valientes picotean
una y otra vez al invasor

quisiera ayudar a los pequeños

mi desesperanza es tan grande
como el pecho del rapaz

en lo alto de un árbol
vemos como posa
la ley del más fuerte

the moon sometimes stays
we see her in the distance
alien to the globalization
of her rosy crater

Suddenly
we all stop for a racket
a revolt of birds against a hawk
pinned immovable in a tree
boasting the steel of his eyes

the anxious little birds
throw themselves against him

"You're frightening my baby"
they seem to say
bravely pecking
the intruder over and over

I would like to help the little ones

my despair is as wide
as the raptor's chest

high up in a tree
we see how the law
of the jungle perches

# Tortugas Marinas

*A mi amiga Raiza*

Esperábamos guiar a las tortugas
desde la arena hacia la mar

la luna nos acompañaba

la más pequeñita rotaba sus aletas
en la tela del aire

supimos entonces

que la arena se iluminaría

que oiríamos el canto del mar

que en el océano
una tortuga es un millón

que la vulnerabilidad
con la que andan
es solamente fe

En un paisaje azul
evitando el peligro
navegarían con el mar

como las mariposas y las aves
o cualquiera de nosotros
las tortugas marinas
hacen de la emigración
su más cálido abrigo

# Sea turtles

*To my friend Raiza*

We were waiting to guide the hatchlings
from the sand toward the sea

the moon was with us

the smallest one rotated its flippers
on the fabric of the air

we knew then

that the sand would light up

that we would hear the sea singing

that in the ocean
one turtle is a million

that the vulnerability
of the way they go
is only faith

In a blue landscape
avoiding danger
they would sail with the sea

like butterflies and bees
or any one of us
sea turtles
make of emigration
their warmest shelter

## Patti Smith

Sandy, de Hollywood, Florida
parecida a Patti Smith
(a quien siempre he querido entrevistar)
fue mi vecina por un tiempo

hablaba mirando hacia otra parte
como expandiendo los pliegues de un espejo
en donde siempre encontraba a su gata

tenía la sonrisa
el pelo largo y blanco
y la nariz de Patti Smith

dibujaba armoniosa con sus manos
el lento paso de un caballo
que acariciaba en Búfalo
su ciudad natal

me enseñaba inglés

compartíamos
los mismos archipiélagos

leyendo a Emily Dickinson
en su idioma
yo en el mío
nos entendíamos en lenguas

## Patti Smith

Sandy, from Hollywood, Florida
resembling Patti Smith
(who I have always wanted to interview)
was my neighbor for a while

she talked looking aside
as if expanding the folds of a mirror
in which she always found her cat

she had the smile
the long white hair
and the nose of Patti Smith

she drew gracefully with her hands
the slow pace of a horse
she was stroking in Buffalo
her native city

she taught me English

we shared
the same archipelagoes

reading Emily Dickinson
in her language
I in mine
we understood each other in tongues

distante, amable y silenciosa
como el que conoce y ama
la ronda de la hierba

llevo su voz como el arete
de esos cálidos días en Florida

mi andar titubeante de extranjera
amaba entrar en su jardín
tomar té con los poetas
y estar cerca de Patti Smith.

distant kind and quiet
like one who knows and loves
the round of the grass

I wear her voice like the earring
of those warm days in Florida

my foreigner's halting gait
loved to enter her garden
take tea with the poets
and be near Patti Smith.

## El sentido del mundo

Alguien tocó la puerta

no iba a abrir

traducía destellos

pero miré por la ventana

y caía
una lluvia de estrellas blancas
que dibujaban
el sentido del mundo

mi tercera nevada en Boston

hubo una gran pausa

la nieve

generativa

fractal

elegante

abría sus cortinas

# The meaning of the world

Someone knocked on the door

I wasn't going to open it

I was translating glimmers

but I looked out of the window

and a shower of white stars
was falling
and drawing
the meaning of the world

my third snowfall in Boston

there was a great pause

the snow

generative

fractal

elegant

was opening its curtains

## Templanza

El torbellino del mundo
nos trae el contratiempo
y la templanza.

En el océano
las tortugas
fusionan su nado con el mar
y emerge el hilo imantado
que las devolverá
a su arena de origen

La luna cambia sus fases
y aparece en el mundo
una migración de mariposas

Aquí
en mi arena movediza
contemplo
extensiones y extensiones
de crepúsculos y lilas

el horizonte comienza
a modular una canción

la cantaremos juntas

# Fortitude

The maelstrom of the world
brings us setbacks
and fortitude.

In the ocean
turtles
blend their swimming with the sea
and the magnetized thread emerges
that will return them
to the sand of their origin

The moon changes its phases
and in the world appears
a migration of butterflies

Here
on my shifting sand
I contemplate
expanses and expanses
of twilights and lilacs

the horizon begins
to modulate a song

we will sing it together

**Nidia Hernández** was born in Venezuela and has been living in the US since 2018. She is a poet, translator of Portuguese poetry, editor, broadcaster, and radio producer. Her editorial project *lamajadesnuda.com* won the 2011 world Summit Awards, and her radio program (also called *La Maja Desnuda*) has presented works from the last 35 years with more than 1,820 broadcasts. Currently, she is broadcasting the program through UPV

*photo by Andrés Manner*

Radio 102.5 FM Spain. She curates *Poesiaudio* (Arrowsmith Press), is a co-editor for *Mercurius Magazine,* a UK publication based in Barcelona, Spain, and belongs to the Board of Directors of New England Poetry Club. Hernández is the winner of the 2021 Sundara Ramaswamy Prize for her editorial work on *The Land of Mild Light* by Rafael Cadenas. In 2022, she published a new anthology, *The Invisible Borders of Time: Five Female Latin American Poets*, for which she won the 2023 Mass Poetry Community Award.


**Rowena Hill** was born in England in 1938, and went to school in New Zealand. She attended universities in New Zealand, Italy and India (University of Mysore). She taught English Literature at the Universidad de Los Andes in Mérida, Venezuela, where she has lived for forty-eight years. She has published six books of poems in Spanish: *Celebraciones, Ida y Vuelta, Legado de*

*Sombras, No es tarde para alabar, Planta baja del cerebro/ Ground Floor of the Brain* (bilingual), *Marea tardía/ Late Tide* (bilingual), and the bilingual selected poems *Rastrojos* (Alliteration, Miami, 2023) as well as poems, essays and translations in periodicals in Venezuela, Colombia, India, USA, and online. She has translated into English some of Venezuela's best-known poets, including Rafael Cadenas, Eugenio Montejo, and Yolanda Pantin.

## Books by

## A R R O W S M I T H PRESS

*Girls* by Oksana Zabuzhko

*Bula Matari/Smasher of Rocks* by Tom Sleigh

*This Carrying Life* by Maureen McLane

*Cries of Animals Dying* by Lawrence Ferlinghetti

*Animals in Wartime* by Matiop Wal

*Divided Mind* by George Scialabba

*The Jinn* by Amira El-Zein

*Bergstein*
edited by Askold Melnyczuk

*Arrow Breaking Apart* by Jason Shinder

*Beyond Alchemy* by Daniel Berrigan

*Conscience, Consequence: Reflections on Father Daniel Berrigan*
edited by Askold Melnyczuk

*Ric's Progress* by Donald Hall

*cont...*

*The Forbidden Door: The Selected Poetry of Lasse Söderberg*
tr. by Lars Gustaf Andersson & Carolyn Forché

*Unrevolutionary Times* by Houman Harouni

*Between Fury & Peace: The Many Arts of Derek Walcott*
edited by Askold Melnyczuk

*The Burning World* by Sherod Santos

*Today is a Different War: Poetry of Lyudmyla Khersonska*
tr. by Olga Livshin, Andrew Janco, Maya Chhabra, & Lev Fridman

*Salvage* by Richard Kearney

*In the Hour of War: Poetry From Ukraine*
edited by Carolyn Forché and Ilya Kaminsky

*A Crash Course in Molotov Cocktails: Poetry of Halyna Kruk*
tr. by Amelia Glaser and Yuliya Ilchuk

*Don't Close Your Eyes* by Hanna Melnyczuk

*Tiny Extravaganzas* by Diane Mehta

*Departures from Rilke* by Steven Cramer

*On the Road to Lviv* by Christopher Merrill
tr. into Ukrainian by Nina Murray

*Nothing Bad Has Ever Happened*
A Bouquet to Victoria Amelina

ARROWSMITH is named after the late William Arrowsmith, a renowned classics scholar, literary and film critic. General editor of thirty-three volumes of *The Greek Tragedy in New Translations*, he was also a brilliant translator of Eugenio Montale, Cesare Pavese, and others. Arrowsmith, who taught for years in Boston University's University Professors Program, championed not only the classics and the finest in contemporary literature, he was also passionate about the importance of recognizing the translator's role in bringing the original work to life in a new language.

*Like the arrowsmith who turns his arrows straight and true,*
*a wise person makes his character straight and true.*

— Buddha

www.ingramcontent.com/pod-product-compliance
Lightning Source LLC
Chambersburg PA
CBHW020356130626
46549CB00006B/2299